Dear Rachael,

Flow with that pen!

Iain Dryden

"Everyone needs to find a way to be in the moment, to find a restorative state that allows them to put down their burdens." Laura Kubzansky, Associate Professor, Human Development and Health, Harvard.

Tracing the Flow

Doodling to unwind.

Iain Dryden

An informed awareness of our senses and emotions leads us from a faux notion of who we are towards a realisation of what we are.* Being both mentally stimulating and physically active, doodling, aided by 'Settling', creates a reliable mindset which enhances this process.

* The central theme of Dan Goleman's inspiring book, 'Emotional Intelligence'.

CONTENTS

The 'activities' start on P.14, but do read P.10-13.

Certain pages herein might seem empty; that's intentional, periodic space helps the mind settle into the process.

Dedicated to Matthew Thompson, who believed in this book. Matthew, who trained hopeful young Olympiads, died unduly young.

PREAMBLE

With each passing year our lives speed up. To keep pace we work and play harder; it is not surprising that we are tainted with tension and zing with a subtle current of anxiety. Yet there were times when we felt free, when life inspired us, when clarity was one thought away.

Be assured, these short, effective sessions based on scientific research can help you regain control and find inner calm. Emergency workers, athletes and people working under extreme duress create a mindset termed The Flow (or in slang, The Zone) into which they slip whenever needed. Think 'Hussain Bolt'.

"But by doodling?" you may ask. Skills involving your hands directly engage the brain.

Doodling is ideal because it can be done anywhere, it is also enjoyable and a happier mind de-stresses more quickly. When coupled to a simple concentrating exercise called 'Settling', doodling becomes a powerful tool.

These sessions work for many reasons, some biological, others intellectual, some psychological, others emotional.

Once we take charge of ourselves, we see the world afresh; we think differently, we act more responsibly consequently people treat us differently.
Our lives feel brighter.

STRESS

Stress arose as a survival tool, it kept us from the lion's jaws. Unfortunately, modern life has too many snarling cats; battered by problems, pressured by time, overburdened by excessive demands, the flight or fight reaction inside us is continuously activated. This generates a cocktail of chemicals. The heart speeds up, muscles receive blood from the gut, our pupils constrict to focus on our "attacker", the bronchi in our lungs increase blood oxygenation and stored energy is used for strength, chemicals such as cortisol linger, making us feel amiss.

This impairs our immune system's responses. Continual stress induces insomnia, a lack of clarity, weakened memory, poor concentration, it mars decision making, anxiety increases, depression arises, even heart disease can occur.

There are many ways of getting rid of such toxins. Try convincing your boss that pirouetting around your desk hitting tennis balls whilst singing with headphones on is good work-practice. It is safer to scribble attentively on a scrap of paper. Artists, scientists, anyone mastering a skill Flows; children do frequently.

Lurking inside us is talent supreme.
Without our intervention, the heart beats, the stomach churns, our thoughts roll on. Furthermore, the mind-body relationship is astounding. One famous bodybuilder won competitions by telling his rivals, seconds before judging, that they looked unprepared. Emotionally unbalanced, they stopped Flowing and their solid surface muscles turned slightly flabby.

Hitch doodling to 'Settling' and you have a potent ally. Settling is simple - it elegantly combines Flowing, practical aspects of Mindfulness and a proven breathing exercise. If resolute, with these transferable skills you should enjoy tranquillity of mind at work and in your home.

SETTLING

This daily exercise is best practised in a quiet place.
In three weeks, when you are adept, 'Settling' can be
done anywhere, (even secretly at work).

Stand tall
Admire your body as a sculpture.
Regardless of your view of it, no work of art is as magnificent.
Extend
arms high (behind your head at work) take a deep belly-breath.
Hold
Slowly Exhale
Repeat 6 times
Lower your arms.

End tall & immerse yourself in a joyous memory,
(a sunny picnic; a wedding day; a holiday; reaching a mountain top).
Smile
and chuckle, knowing this positive, strong person is you.
Aren't you great!
Say, "I'm fine!"

Attention is key.
Fix this new mindset by briefly focusing, be it in the
shower or on the bus. At work 'Settling' briefly can help
you meet a hectic deadline. When walking home,
hesitate and be safe in this new natural space. Like any
activity, the more you practice, the better you'll get.
Repeated actions become effortless habits, but stop them
for four days and they are difficult to restart, because the
short-cut chain has been broken and needs recreating.
It only takes three months to engrain an attitude.

intro-ish

THE SOOTHING SYSTEM

The vagus nerve, part of the involuntary nervous system, connects the brain to the lungs, digestive tract, heart and other organs. It controls subconscious activity such as the heart beat and is responsible for the fight or flight response.

Importantly, the vagus system also soothes your body after moments of stress, letting it return to its vital work. It can be irritated by anguish, poor posture, alcohol, stress, anxiety and fatigue. Healthy vagal tone accompanies physical and mental wellbeing, weak tone is associated with depression, negative moods, heart attacks, and stroke.

Current research has found that six deep-belly breaths with a very slow exhale stimulates the vagus nerve, slowing the heart rate, lowering blood pressure, inducing a state of mental calm. Midwives encourage women in labour to breathe in this manner to manage pain and focus on the birthing process.

Children naturally have a strong vagal tone. Adults with strong vagal tone are active, healthy and positive, they produce more insulin, hence suppress inflammation more easily. Positive emotions, robust social connections and physical health influence one another in a self-sustaining dynamic feedback loop. Studies show vagal tone improves with exercise and, amazingly, when we reflect upon positive emotions and experiences.

By combining Vagal Breathing, positive emotional memories and mindful attention, 'Settling' is an effective exercise.

HOW TO USE THIS BOOK

All tasks in this book are do-able, given patience plus a tint of joy, for this combination soothes anxiety and generates immersion, which creates a sense of well-being. Research shows these undemanding activities brighten your attitude (and your attitude intensifies the impact of these sessions).

✳ These sessions are not another task to get done, they are a treat you have decided to give yourself. Developing an innocent and attentive mindset is key, furthermore, this process will only work when you take your time.

✳ Spend no less than a day per section, maybe more, and if determined, if you have fun, these activities ought to engrain a new mindset within 3 weeks. Develop this over 3 months and these new skills should continually enchant you.

✳ Buy cheap sketchbooks, pencils, pens, a medium width watercolour brush and tube of grey watercolour paint for the exercise on P. 79. Spending little money will free you and stop your doodles becoming precious, for they are little more than the vehicle.

✳ Keep these doodle books secret until confident!

as 4 intros, well… that's it (Joy) …at last…

THE POWER OF WORDS

Start each session Settling, Smiling*and telling yourself,
"I'm fine!"

Breathe deeply, flex your fingers and wrist, pick up a
pencil.

LETTERS. It might seem bizarre to begin with writing, but
when young we put huge effort into learning this
remarkable skill. Doodle lazy letters, marvelling at
simple lines and curves which convey so much. Alter the
pencil pressure and its angle, creating changes in tone
and density of hue. Try logos of your initials.

Here's mine

my wife's are nicer

WORDS. Advertisers know words are powerful. Smile
and each evening write positive key-words about your
day and your relations.

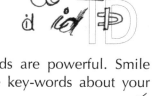

You can do better
I'm su

I ¹⁴ D

doodling doodling doodling
dabbling
doodling doodling
dallying
doodling

Did you say dawdling?

... maybe in a refined manner?

hmm !

there are no rules but this : SMILE

*
SMILING triggers the brain reward system more than winning on the horses. Even forced smiling, which uses 30 muscles, positively stimulates the brain (another of Newton's suspicions proven right). Smiles make you more attractive. Smiling you are taken as competent. There's even a correlation between the broadness of people's smiles and the length of their lives.

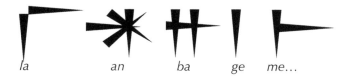

la   an   ba   ge   me…

Sumerian script.

Sumerians invented writing roughly 5,500 years ago, ingeniously condensing pictograms into repetitive marks. They understood words are knowledge distilled. Words store information, illuminate the past, direct actions and reveal effective solutions.

MRI scans show cortisol is produced when we hear or say the word 'No'; it takes three slow, attentive repetitions of 'Yes' to counter this negative effect. Words affect our reactions. Hearing yourself called 'Idiot' instead of 'Cool' sets off related cellular activity. In 2015, Facebook manipulated words in feeds, influencing how a million customers wrote to each other. Furthermore, self-directed words are engrained - calling yourself useless can make you clumsy and, well, perhaps a little useless. MRI scans also show writing positive key-words about your day, relationships and yourself helps those suffering from anxiety and depression. Making these visually interesting requires positive attention and creativity, boosting the effect - so keep doodling.

comfort care bloom best
able accept
celebrate adore
appreciate
bright altruistic
create
happiness
considerate
delight   decent
empathy   friendly
generous good   health   honest   inspire
integrity **jolly** kiss life noble OK open
positive

quiet ripe radiant serene smart trust **tender**
unique   vim   well   Xanadu   youth
joy
zeal

2
THE AMAZING THUMB

Settling. Enjoy your breath's rhythm, sensing regenerative oxygen entering your body. Watch the waves created in your chest, the subtle lifting of your shoulders and abdomen. Being aware of your body's sensations helps you briefly disentangle from thought's gripping currents.

Riding this tranquil awareness, slip into your writing-fingers. Immerse yourself in each muscle, feeling their swell. Trace your splayed fingers, marvelling at the subtle changes of line which add up to their shape. Accept inaccuracies, for artistic perfectionism screws this system as we free ourselves from the fear of drawing which most of us picked up when aged about 11.

Move the page to the table's edge, trace the thumb and fore finger laid flat. Blake and Michelangelo didn't paint this extraordinary pincer movement for nothing. It is eminently human. Indian mudras, popularised by the Buddha's peace sign, recognise its significance. What does it mean to you?

Trace different spreads of fingers and 5mm from these lines, enjoy repeating the bends and loops. Doodle carefully, pensively, again and again, flipping the pages until you are relaxed in the physical process of turning your tracings into something else.

From now on, the curves in hands can embellish your future doodles.

Sometimes images are repeated for the effect pattern produces in our minds. See P. 34.

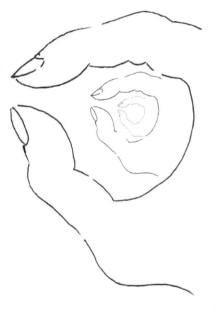

Perfect engineering ensures our fingers work with precision. We knot, grip or stroke them, we point them. Apes' stumpy fingers and palms (which resemble our foot), clench with a full fist when manipulating twig tools, stick weapons and crushing stones. Gradually the simple thumb-forefinger gesture, which humans alone make, evolved, granting us precise manipulation. Another evolutionary refinement, the nerve clumps at each finger's end, give us incredible sensitivity.

This dexterity* stimulated the growth of the frontal cortex and we fashioned, rather than found tools, enhancing our ability to reason. With stone knives and bone needles to work animal skins, we migrated to colder climes. We lit fires, marked cave walls. Significantly, amongst our earliest images are prints of our amazing hands. We went on to doodle elephants, humans, horses. We made flutes and drums, we danced to our musical compositions.

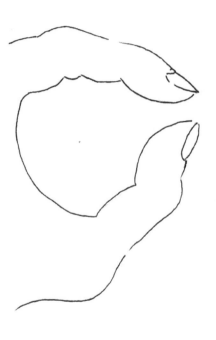

Our developing hand-brain relationship enabled us to make bricks, build cities. We fashioned pens, intricate jewellery, turned steering wheels, manipulated touch-screens. We wrote novels, soared to the moon and today we hold nature's fate in our hands.

Relish massage-rubbing these extraordinary creations. By sprinkling joyous 1-3 minutes doodling moments across your day, everything but what you are doing will eventually drop away.

*Try spending 5 minutes doodling thumbless, or using a key to open a door, but perhaps not on your bike as you'd fall off !

3
MIRACULOUS ATTENTION

Settled? Slowly breathe, relax, breathe as you doodle. Admire your sculptural body, feel how sensitive your finger-skin is. Run them across the paper. Keenly sense the pressure you exert when using the pencil. The wood tickles your skin, enjoy its firmness.

Let's enrich your work with basic techniques you used in childhood. Trace your finger shapes. Around them doodle marks and smudges. Angle the pencil for a sleek or fat line. Generate different effects, experimenting, discovering what you feel suits each shape. Yes, feel! Moving dramatically, learn to engage your emotions, for this is our game.

As we breathe, oxygen enters the blood through the alveoli in our lungs and the heart quickens, carrying red blood cells to our organs, bones and tissues. The heart slows as we breathe out, ridding us of carbon dioxide; this is controlled by the vagus nerve.

The way we breathe relates to our mood. Often when working we tense and hold our breath, affecting the internal processes; the body assumes we are threatened, stress increases. Soldiers are trained to breathe naturally, for when panicked we snap air in and out, when calm our breath is longer, slower.

In deep sleep the parasympathetic system slows our breathing to 3 per minute and this is when the body heals damaged cells. Likewise, when we are relaxed, our breath is slower and our body soothes itself with its curing processes.

Although it is usually best to allow your breath to find it's own level, when strained we need a helping hand. Taking deep vagal breaths in times of difficulty helps us focus and disengage from the tendency to react. It prompts blood to flow more easily, and the extra oxygen eases the body's systems, which helps relax us.

Powerful people are more assertive, less stressed, more opportunistic. Research shows that a manager who isn't weak and sufficiently dominant generally rises the ladder quicker than one who is good natured, intelligent or efficient. It comes down to basics - if there's a tough work problem, many would rather the former ruled.

yes, strange, but true...

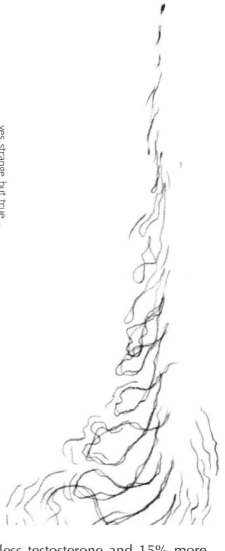

African tribal people stand tall, walk elegantly erect, are balanced. Even faking works, so stand tall, body suspended from your crown and you'll feel great. Posture not only defines how we are seen, research shows that posture alters what is happening inside us. Stand tall for only two minutes and there's 20% more testosterone and 25% less stressing cortisol in the blood. Slouch and that's 10% less testosterone and 15% more cortisol. Testosterone, in small doses, is beneficial.

PAT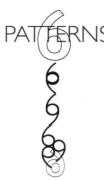RNS

A pounding heart isn't necessarily a sign of anxiety, so relax and link your hands behind your neck, stretch the elbows back, arch your back and neck, breathe slowly in and out, feel your body move; love being alive.

Let's be inspired by ancient tribal symbols. To the left are traditional representations of stars. On the right, a collection of abstract patterns strung together. Symbols are an almost universal language used since the dawn of cultural evolution.

Don't attempt to be precise, these images are purposefully rough.

Create your own symbols for things and characters around you. Make such designs part of your doodles. Search the internet for ideas - leaf patterns, natural forms, anything which catches you. Remember, loose sketching is an uncritical form of communication.

A PATTERN OR TWO

6

The brain seeks patterns to understand the world and art abounds in patterns. That patterns are an intellectual expression of the deep mind has long been confirmed in interviews with tribal artists (Aboriginal, North American, African). Children incessantly draw, depicting things important to them. In adults, this specifically human pastime is frequently blocked by rational thought's dominance.

Patterns can also be life-styles. There are too many tantalising patterns to confuse us - financial success? Glossy career? Vast house? Sexy car? Gadgets galore? We need homes, money and satisfying work, but what worth are these if we do not feel fulfilled? The trick is to see what satisfies you long-term and reach towards positive life patterns.

As I drew, I realised her mental pattern wasn't at odds with her reality. Poor as a mouse, yet calm as a sage, your life can still be rich. Her smile was beatific, though she squatted before her cardboard home. She cooked curry on open flames for her infants who teased windblown rubbish upon an oily roadside puddle. Impoverished as she was, she refused my money. Her radiance was unforgettable.

7
ABSTRACTION

Settle, effortlessly breathe and feel composed. Squint absently at the world, seeing it as a flat canvas, a distorted Picasso, a mathematical Mondrian.

Distort and play with the 2D shapes you see, doodling all sorts of fantasy creations which are your own take. Allow your pencil to discover them, let the mind take a back seat. These here happen to be soothing curls, yours could be angular or blocky, but make them yours as you roll your dreamy marks about the page, creating images as small or as big as you like. Sensually decorate them with marks, patterns, dots.

Stretch, breathe it into your fingers and on to the page. Think of the release and gratification this is giving you. Yes! You are allowed to feel delight.

7

Nobel

Nobel

Nobel Prize winners are 15 times more likely to engage in art & craft activities than the general population, illustrating the link between creative abstraction and break-through theories. The best art expresses abstract feelings and thought.

Our ancestors' marks - dots, lines, circles and rectangles, portrayed abstract thought. Abstraction allowed us to refine guttural noises into language and so ideas spread between clans and tribes, eventually forming regional cultures.

Adept at abstraction, we hold complex thoughts together in working memory and create things. Inventing involves strategic thinking, problem solving, planning and innovation, permitting us, for example, to make animal traps. Trust your fingers to produce abstractions, knowing the body reflects the brain.

Nobel

9
CLICK

After Settling, be aware of the shades and colours surrounding you, allow your mind to favourably compare them and decide which pleases you most. Flit your eyes about, rapidly registering various objects, mentally snap-shooting them as if for the first time.

Marvel that you can see the mug on your table so clearly because your eye defines, your mind refines and your brain interprets. Look at the relationship between its height and width, note the curve of its circular top, its handle, its designs (if any). Doodle with relaxed intent, making your lines faint. Don't make perfect ovals or lines straight - you are doodling, not aiming to be the next Vermeer, well, not yet.

If you become too serious, laugh* and go 'Hippie' on design. This will transport you back to those hallowed days before our muddled teens when most of us fooled about with shapes. You may 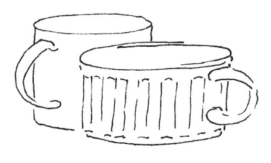 wish to add a bit of shading to give the impression of roundness.

Our brains prioritise vision for a good reason. Niftily summarising events in pictures is a vital survival tool. You see the grass shiver and imagine a snake, not a cuddly puppy. If it turns out to be the former when you thought of the puppy, you'd better run.

*Laughter isn't primarily associated with humour. It is a bonding noise which existed before jokes. Apes laugh as they tumble about, as do children play-fighting with their parents.

When working with the traumatised after wars or tsunamis have devastated their lives, therapists ask people to take mental 'snap-shots' of positive images every few minutes - a flower, a cloud, light on that roof, and to pause and appreciate these things. When this becomes habitual, it gradually helps to regulate emotions and hence deeply shocked minds revive. Moreover, labelling feelings, making them part of a story is not only cathartic, but has been found to affect our immune systems.

If positive snap-shots help, imagine the power of transforming such images into rapid doodles! Look - that jar, that pen - every shape is fascinating. Really. If not, it's you, not the object at fault.

Yet retaining purely positive thoughts diminishes our ability to form accurate reality checks.
We thus form warped memories of incidents, which leads to our memory stores becoming less reliable.

10
GESTURES

Having Settled, fix your visual attention on various part of your body, - the curve of your shoulder, give it a shrug; an elbow, flick it; flex your wrist; give your hand a stretch.

Appreciate your curved shoes. Doodle them with easy movements of your hand.

Allow your pencil to flourish, creating other curves and circles, here - fruit and vegetables. No detail, simply enjoyable arcs.

Smile as you work. Admire that cherry or pepper, think of its taste, of how it grew and cherish it.

Using lazy lines, remember that images never capture reality, the word 'cherry' isn't the juicy flesh.

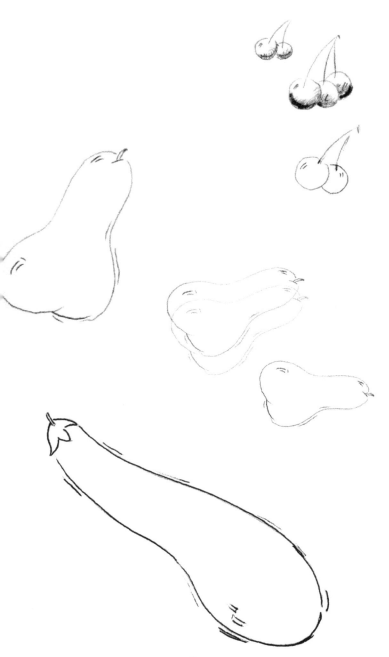

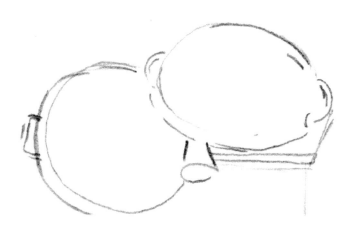

Gestures are an engrained trait, great apes use between 60-100 to communicate and human infants share many of these until language's syntax subsumes them. Even city dwellers understand many ape gestures, yet the meaning of specific gestures can change between cultures, take the V sign. Scientists have shown that using gestures whilst learning something new helps engrain the experience. When we wave to a friend, electricity vitalises a specific part of the brain.

An analysis of TED Talk videos found the most popular were those in which speakers used calm hand gestures at chest height. However, excessive-gesturing and 'jazzy' hands were less liked.

Doodling is full of subtle gestures, as is writing. Studies have compared people making notes, those who write, rather than type, absorb more, for writers condense and synthesise ideas rather than simply record them and writing's subtle gesturing reinforces what they assimilate.

When doodling you actively blend emotions, technical judgements, ideas and aesthetic values. A sense of aesthetics is a basic human trait, across the world, no cultural group is without art.

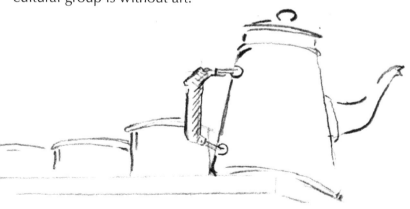

Try this with a light pencil, bolden afterwards with a pen.

11
DISTRACTION

Tense? Most of us are, due to tough lives, unfair demands, sick or ageing bodies. Incredibly, simple acceptance of our condition, rather than fighting it, enables us to appreciate life's little joys. Settle and feel the skin of your cheeks and lips.

How is your mouth - smiling, tight or open? Move it around, creating amusing shapes as if you were humouring a child.

Buy a comic and, like children do, copy various mouths. You'll soon find yourself entertained and you'll be in great company - Goya, David Hockney and most great artists learned through copying other artists.

Mouths are a great way to catch character. Look up and notice the variety of emotions on the mouths near you - that client over there, your slippery colleague, somebody you like, (even desire). Litter your page with moody mouths, angry mouths, happy mouths, munching mouths. But be aware - you might find your own mouth mimicking the image you are creating.

Silly doodling is a great way to ease you from the strains of the moment - your train might be late or the task you are involved in is going wrong. Because it momentarily distracts you and it requires amused attention, it helps balance your mood.

Mouths express so much and are used in different ways in each culture. Keralans in India consider pointing at a third person rude, so pucker their lips towards the individual. The French pucker charmingly, but generally their mouth movements aren't as wide as Spaniards', the English minimalise lip movement; but there are exceptions everywhere.

Creating a new mindset by mimicking an amusing mouth can be a helpful distraction. Mothers frequently change a raging child's mindset by alerting them to something that will interest them. When being treated without painkillers by a traditional surgeon, people in Tibet take their minds off the pain by intensely visualising a 'Mandala' (a concentric design centring on Buddha).

When in a muddle, distract yourself with something silly or positive and smile at yourself, gaining a little healthy self-detachment. By keeping a clear vision of what we are up to, we can gradually change our views. Peace of mind resides inside us, even when the going gets tough, you can generally plug in.

Dubious? Read the tale on P. 126.

12
AMAZING EYES

When there's time, briefly running through the senses will dislocate you from thought's diversions. Not that thought is bad, it is simply inappropriate to lock in to it when you wish to relax.

In a cafe, park, railway station, Settle, listen to the sounds wafting about you as if they were music. Seek exciting eyes. Wide-eyed, slit-eyed, sad-eyed, crazy eyed? Joyous eyes? Doodle, feeling the mood of each eye-expression you capture and chuckle.

Drifting past flowers sprinkled with sun, the innocent eye sparks inside you. Allow it to flit around your thoughts, twinkling the world with magic. This is no romance. Letting enchantment enter his consciousness enabled Van Gogh to rise above turgid, untalented works and explore which led him to create stunning paintings.

Realise how lucky you are. People dodging bullets, sewer-rats or freezing under plastic tents would dance with devils to have this luxury we take for granted. Others, too sick (physically or mentally), are unable to be this appreciative of their environment.

Here are eyes from tribal images.

Few creatures have only one eye and spiders have eight; horses' eyes, on the side of their heads, grant 350 degree vision; dogs only see clearly up to about 6-7 metres and cats have better night vision than us, but beyond light pollution, we can spot a candle 30 miles away. Even though sharks see 10x better under water, we can see stars light-years away, and we clearly define at arms length a grid of lines 60x60 printed on our fingernail. We can also see roughly 1,000,000 colour hues.

We compute distance because we have two eyes. Try navigating a cluttered room or a busy pavement with one eye closed. Our eye is designed to swivel and focus and when we scan the horizon for threats and opportunities, our pupils are wide; upon seeing something, they close down to pick through the light-shade detail, analysing the subject. People living in the wilds of Africa instantly spot a far off lion, yet urban tourists have generally lost this skill because we hardly scan or focus more than a hundred metres away as we drive or walk.

We judge others by retina movement, normally 3-5 flicks per second - slow and somebody's sleepy; lack of eye contact can signal autistic traits. Kathakali actors in Southern India convey emotion with eye movements. This is formalised by ordinary people in Kerala, it is quite an art. The eye sends messages to the brain, the mind distorts these to suit our mental make-up and we believe the internal imagery we've created, (a rope becomes a snake!). That roof over there looks straight, the builder sees it needs repairing; that hill looks big, the mountaineer sees a pimple; this table seems solid, to a scientist it is atoms with huge gaps between them. That person's smiling eyes warm you but your neighbour sees them as an 'oily-eyed' smirk.

13
MULTI-TASKING

Once you have Settled, hold up a hand-mirror and keep looking at your face. There is harmony in its proportions. Your eyes are roughly half way down your head, the pupils are approximately as far apart as the length of your nose, which is vaguely the width of your mouth.

Mentally holding these approximate proportions, lightly line in a mouth, dot in eyes, strike a nose, create a curve for the top of the head. If satisfied, 'bold it'. Whoopee! You've almost doodled a face! Stand up, do a jig, for this activity makes even adults happy.

Run through frowns, smiles, laughs, squints and more, six at the same time, multi-facing. Put on your favourite music, rapping away with your non-drawing hand, humming, wiggling your legs, shifting about chair-dancing. It'll make the activity more fun, (maybe not in the office). There we are, more multitasking! Add more actions - keep looking at things out the window, hone in on conversations, mentally compare your work to other days' doodlings.

Multi-tasking? Well, no.
Attention is total, not scattered.
So called 'Multi-tasking' is switching between mental processes and juggling 4-5 task-balls is normal (walk, talk, screen-scroll, greet somebody, smile, sigh at somebody else, step off the pavement, oops)… whee… with each shift taking milli-seconds. Shifting back and forth between goals costs more than the sum of these actions, because the mental gymnastics and the 'executive' ranking and assessing employed are consumptive as cells pulse electrical signals to hubs which enable long range connectivity between diverse, sometimes conflicting, mental regions. Phwee, see!

Each new or infrequent thing forms mental task-chains containing many links, to save energy frequent actions (walking) are miraculously bundled into a single link; this also enables rapid action when required. When juggling 5+ tasks, the overloaded mind assumes we are threatened and produces cortisol and adrenaline, inhibiting normal brain activity so as to confront the imagined threat, resulting in 40% less cognitive effectiveness. Drained, we push harder to keep juggling, costing more energy and stress mounts!

Recalling an intensely positive moment from your past, fix the associated video in your mind. Daily returning to it (when Settling), increases the electricity in the brain cells which store it, hence making it more powerful, endorphins are released, a little helpful testosterone too. Total attention reaps its reward, enhancing the effects.

15
THE MENTAL GYM

Settle into your body. Become aware of the form it has taken - leaning against a bus shelter, slouched in your office chair, is your torso spread across the dining table? Imagine your shadow projected upon a cave wall. Look at these graceful cave paintings, done with an easy eye, a touch of humour and an uncomplicated understanding of the human shape. We are not that different to our doodling ancestors, they lacked our technology but were probably as emotionally and intellectually sensitive as we are.

Doodling cartoon faces ought to have evaporated drawing-fear and you'll find caveman-like figures easy because they are almost random shapes, so you can invent your own rules!

Have a doodle, allowing ancient artwork to lead you into doodling rapid blobby shapes, expressing what you feel as you create with no fear of failure. Offices, train stations, parks and cafes lend themselves to this covert activity. Be brave, that woman won't know you're exaggerating, nor that man. Go on, dob-on more ink and titter quietly as you catch those who lure your eye. Settle as you Doodle, for it's a doddle.

15

These cave drawings illustrate the brain's ability to sum up visual input without fuss. Creating such easy figures involves playing with and manipulating the pencil and this technical skill engages muscles, nerves and specific brain sectors. Interpreting the 3D human shape onto 2D paper means calculating, defining, refining and then there's the construction skills.

It takes abstract thinking to hold all this together and allow these impressions to flow along your pencil and out onto the paper. Making them please your eye involves a dozen other mindsets dealing with values, judgements, acceptance, aesthetics... and accepting mistakes as part of the learning process. OK, energy consumptive, but undertaken one step at a time, a soothing mental-workout.

There we are - a little more proof that fooling around with a pencil is more than merely being productive. Doodling's impressive.

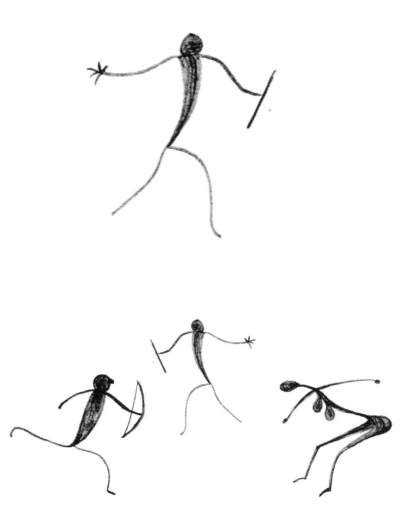

16
BEING PLAYFUL

Settle. Fingers blocking your ears, relish the sound streaming within you - breath, heartbeat, blood-flow. Let go and listen outside, be it a whirring computer, radio or birdsong. Sound quickly puts us in the moment. Sound reaches us in our last moments. If you are listening to life's music as you doodle, not planning or fretting, today's task should be entertaining.

Doodling fluid stick folk is not about learning anatomical proportions, but watching people as you scribble. See, her shoulders take the weight as she leans against the wall; the young dude dancing looks like he'll topple over. Accuracy is not a problem, note the man hammering. Go on to create cartoon-stories involving several stick folk.

If accuracy interests you, it will gradually arise with practice as your eye-to-hand coordination improves and particularly if you let it happen*. Never judge yourself harshly. All artists have periods when they 'get it' and days, weeks even, when they don't.

Conjure up your inner child by doodling with your tongue in your cheek, or (if alone) stick it out. Children spend hours doodling, it hones their motor skills and exercises many mental attributes. For many of us, carefree existence ended with childhood, so play, it helps unwind.

*If so, spend 2-4 weeks doing nothing but cave and stick folk.

Children don't generally fuss as they doodle, but amuse themselves. As children we were alert, intuitive, analytical, experimental, in other words, probably more intelligent than we are now. Play, which is experimentation, endowed our children with mental plasticity and curiosity, enabling abstraction, art, reflection, analysis and reasoned planning, granting us an advantage over other species. Neanderthals' shorter childhoods created smaller prefrontal cortexes and practical 'young adults', whereas the extended human childhood develops this brain region responsible for reasoning, social behaviour and symbolic thought.

Stories are part of play. Imagining future scenarios, we respond in fresh ways to threats and challenges. We transmit this through tales, which bond us, enriches our world view, prepares us for life. Narrative can be pictures on cave walls; words in newspapers, books, the radio, TV and the internet, and is of lost civilisations, the way animals live, what others are up to, revolutionary concepts.

Reaching beyond convention, inventors, creators, entertainers and artists, tap into those springs of wakefulness which lead to cutting-edge ideas. Rodin, Shakespeare, Hokusai, Dylan, their visual or word stories resonate across the decades; how many teachers, soldiers, business people are as respected worldwide?

17
EMOTION

What emotional state were you in before Settling and afterwards? Squeeze a little grey watercolour into a mixing plate, dip your medium width brush into water, shake off excess. Mix one edge of the paint, forming pigment decreasing in intensity the further from the paint it goes. Clean the brush. Lift the lightest hue, dip it onto your paper and watch it spread. Dry it with a hair-drier.

Onto this, sweep paint varying in density to give hard edges. Dry it. Using the brush as a pen add dabs, dots and marks with various potencies of paint. Experiment. Be playful, discover how to create different effects, always drying. Even use your finger print. Keep flipping the pages.

Rapidly breathe fully in-out of your nose five times. No more.

If you feel dizzy (in any situation), don't panic, stop, sit, let your breath return to normal. Panic disturbs the body-mind, even endangering it. Crack troops are taught that in freezing water, panic kills, but by waiting, relaxing, the breath soothes your systems and you survive.

When these pages dry, overlay more paint, weak or strong, creating double, even triple layered effects in places and in others leaving the original washes. Be emotional. Smudge some parts, make others opaque, some translucent.

With a drier mix, make marks and hatch, create lines, relish your emotional creativity.

This game is endless fun.

Emotions are non-verbal, involuntary reactions to situations. They release neuro-chemicals in the brain, increasing or decreasing it's activity, stimulating bodily gestures, postures and movements. Traditionally, emotion is feared, seen to blind reason. Emotion is powerful, it is registered by the same brain receptors which record physical pain, that is why heart break 'hurts'.

We recognise emotional states in others, however, comparative studies show we can't always tell what people from other cultures are feeling as contextual influences portray emotion differently. This implies learning influences moral emotions, and possibly even basic emotion.

Watching emotion allows us to comprehend their mechanism and respond appropriately. Emotion leads us beneath our mental veils and by trusting them, but tempering them with understanding, refines us.

Each society, clan and family has its own emotional customs, consequently your joys, disgusts, angers and sadnesses will be different to your friend's. A bird swooping too close over your pram might have instilled fear because your mother disliked birds, yet it could generate adoration in another. In the African bush, dangerous snakes are a normality, hence are accepted, yet harmless spiders can trigger fear in Europeans. Individuals living with constant external threats often respond more aggressively to the intrusion of others than people used to continual peace. And people on the edge of survival have different emotional values to those used to abundance - understanding people's fundamental milieu will help us lean towards cooperation.

Emotion tints our creativity. Understanding this, Apple products are tactile and logic is driven by intuition, making them fun to use and thus desirable.

18
PLEASURE

After Settling, accept you as you are right now. Cortisol increases when we fight ourselves, as does discomfort. Smile, tell yourself, "I'm fine!" Sense the distance between your fingers and your eyes. Two eyes allow you to measure distance and perspective. Shift your gaze to your foot and 'measure' its distance from your pupils. Admire something a few metres away then 'feel' the distance to a more distant item.

Seek something easy like a bush in a park which is replicated a few times. Rapidly doodle in their outlines, one behind the other, big, smaller, tiny at fifty metres. Congratulations! Perspective took artists centuries to master. Stand up, do a jig!

Making mistakes is part of learning, yet "Getting It Right!" was shoved into our brains at school. Fine in maths but unhelpful when seeking tranquillity. Work lightly, creating the feeling of distance upon flat paper by making the foreground heavier, the middle lighter and the distance faint. Find other objects, a fence, street lamps and fool around, overlaying, doodling, messing about.

School lead us to gain from, rather than enjoy life, yet we are hard-wired to experience pleasure. Babies respond to their parents' smiles, they giggle when certain music plays. Apes dance joyfully upon discovering a jungle waterfall. Uncover the grinning, dancing child-ape within, confident that the brain takes imagined events as real. Aping about pleases and stimulates. When we're pleased, dopamine enters our bloodstream and soon endorphins make us euphoric, we pay less attention to our usual aches and pains. And content, we smile.

Contentment is happiness and we decide what that is - a stimulating relationship, a Zen garden or no garden at all. Short-term happiness is also what we decide - a picnic in the park, a night dancing. Contentment involves being in the moment, multiples of such experiences assist our long term happiness. After all, life happens right now.

Material items are shown not to satisfy for long, whereas positive experiences do. After a while, lottery winners are no happier than before. Happiness arises from successful relationships, being with what is, doing well in one's projects. Sharing or giving generates heaps of happiness. When happy, we touch others with

our unthreatening magnetism, for happiness is contagious. Seeing a great athlete, actor or a stranger bursting with heartfelt joy upon winning an award or getting married, most sane people feel joyous.

Emotional vitality, enthusiasm and engagement, as well as facing life's stresses, seem to reduce the risk of heart disease. Knowing happiness is your own invention, doodle with flourish and litter your life with merry moments. Smiling, a win-win wonder, is addictive and it helps de-stress. Hooked on this high, artists play when in a creative mood, look no further than Wallace & Gromit.

19
SELF IMAGE

Settle and sense your body. Throat relaxed? Shoulders easy? Chest open? Posture erect? Composed, calm, content? Appreciate this moment, whatever it has served up. Love what you are doing, let it warm you, if you can't, maybe change it. Appreciating the moment is purpose enough, it transports, it heals, it makes life worth living.

Pencil doodling part of a building is a ball because, broken down to essentials, it is straight lines. Slowly, avoiding accuracy, observe the structure (a window, a door?), make light marks, bold some of them later. Look - my doodles are rough.

Brush in small grey washes of shadow, texture, depth. Dry the doodles and load the brush with strong drier pigment, dance it across your washes, hatching, dotting, making long or short lines. Whoopie! Do more - chimneys, roofs, perhaps a turret....

As you work, you enrich your days by capturing your world, for it is not only your paper which records these precious moments. What's happening inside is more important. Taking a photo is done with. Doodling, you are there, observing, analysing, understanding, recording, *relishing*.

Pat yourself for getting this far and keep working at this inner task, because sooner than you can imagine it will be too late - all those years, they shot past like arrows.

Patterns of behaviour suiting the archetypical character which external forces coerced us into being, influence how we stand, move our facial muscles, the tune of our voices, the words we choose. Our view of ourselves colours our world view, fuelling the way we react. Reacting from their own archetype, people can reinforce our self image, making us feel socially at ease or awkward. What we assume to be correct influences our characters, enabling us to do, or not to do certain things - climbing a mountain, become a physicist, being open to new people.

One shy person who always upon panicked seeing open water, even from the safety of a beach, was challenged to cross a tranquil pond. They refused. Helped to understand fear is a mental construct, they steeled themselves and grasping a float, they crossed. It was a game-changer, this timid person instantly felt potent. Constantly reinforcing this fresh self-image, they gradually progressed and became a confident character.

Our doodles reflect what we think of ourselves. Sketching the church above, I felt pathetic, having been dropped by a French girlfriend. The previous day when life felt perfect, I did the one below of the famous Parisian cathedral Notre Dame.

Being kind to ourselves, accepting what we are, mistakes and all, chuckling at our weirdness, generates self-empathy, it relaxes our mental sphere, we start to feel more balanced. Our empathy turns outwards, we consider the needs of others, we enjoy life more.

20
CHANGE

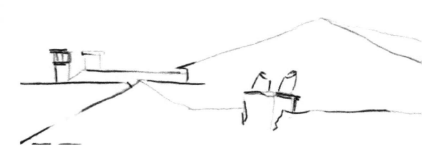

Settle and notice your pulse and breath working to keep you vital. Mentally snap a tiny detail of your surroundings. The brain automatically simplifies ten thousand leaves into a tree's outline. Distance is understood in this way - skylines become simple shapes. Lightly pencil the roofs across the road or that hedge cresting the horizon.

Increasingly heavier marks will add character, perspective, lean on the lead, enhancing that chimney/tree/road. Fool about, starting again and again, drawing, if you must, with the casual touch of the doodler.

Shade, hatch or watercolour wash to your heart's content, not being precious, learning by your little errors, laughing at what your pencil reveals. Art is serendipitous. It is as if magic appears out of nowhere.

Change can only happen once you accept emotion as part of yourself, not something to shun or shame. And change arises once we see that our illusionary self-image was created by an emotional 3 year old child who, in defence against others created this complex suit of faux-armour. Perhaps at the time we needed to become vague to deflect unwanted demands, maybe we toughened up to survive or became jokey to be accepted. Upon facing your infant self, be not alarmed that there's several other wounded selves inside.

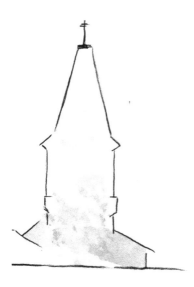

You are not only a psychological jumble of entangled emotions, hunches, reactions, aspirations, but also something physical, something animal. Yes, we smart phone addicts are creatures more inspiring and sturdy, more adaptable and adventurous than we assume we are. Being 'in the body', laying attention in the senses, helps lift you from your self-image's confusing, complex puddles. Choosing to Settle/Doodle permits life's dross to settle*, allowing the cool current lurking behind your self-image to emerge.

Regularly sensing this subtle inner force conjures up an improved self-image based on feeling, not thinking. Stand tall, breathe deep, stretch high! As this mindset engrains itself you can be *what* you are, not *who* you assume you are.

*This is why I chose the term 'Settle'.

21
YOUR INNER SAMURAI

Settle and sigh with a smile, realising your entire life has come to this - YOU as you are this moment. You, the astonishing being beneath those kids and images and complexes. Feel the subtle static inside your hands, chest, face, feet. Stand tall and immerse yourself in YOU. Marvel at this internal vigour, know it is exceptional, that it is alive. That you will never be repeated, in all of time there's only one of you. Yes, you are unique! Despite what is going on in your life, this entity continues hardly noticed. Notice it! Admire it! Love it. Use its force for your own good, for everyone's benefit. There is no better purpose.

A beret fast cyclist

QUICK!

Get your pencil. There's a mad cyclist, cat or bird shooting past. Let go and simply allow the pen do its work. Laugh at the result. OK, it may not be an exact replica, but it has vitality. That's art for you, it ignores conventional limits. What you create is special, it arises from your secret world.

When your pencil responds without interruption to the impulses arising from your eye, your emotions, motor-skills and logic are in harmony with your body. You are in, or posed on the edge of The Zone. Poised in this place, your physical and mental 'selves' are more able to perform at their optimum. That is the athlete's mindset.

If you want, shade your doodlings using any washes or marks you wish. Starting at the darkest point gives a sense of 3D.

Trust your body and your new Settled mindset, ensuring it floats you through life's choppy seas.

Perfecting this inner stillness, Samurai sword masters slice arrows fired directly at them*. When the sword (or pen) is part of the body-consciousness, these apparently magical skills are attainable. Who would have thought anyone would ever run as fast and as smoothly as Hussain Bolt! Feel your inner Samurai, touch your secret resilience and ride life upon your own raft of tranquility.

* Dubious - think of squash champions - how can they see that rapid little ball?

a beret Zen wobble ?

We each have our own wisdom accumulated from a mixture of common sense and emotional responses to situations we've encountered. Each of our world-views are different. Respecting one another's, realising that deep beneath our cultural covers, essential parts of us are roughly alike, we can aim for balanced interactions with less friction and greater empathy.

that's it

...the last session...

...but there's a little more, if you want...

We can each become a beret wise person

A beret noble tribesman

A copy of a rapid old doodle of a man I did in Kenya, where I grew up. I've added the berets at the top. My hero, my mentor, my greatest friend, was a gentle yet fearless and noble Nandi warrior called Kipchebet, (see P. 126). (…and the berets? Also see P. 126)

Beware!

Don't sink into the # doodle

doldrums

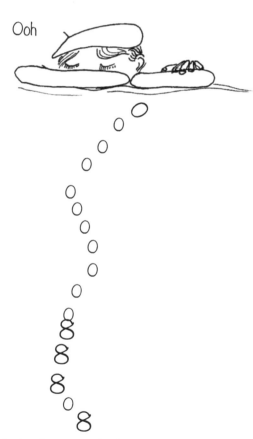

Ooh

...so to help, here's **8** little extras to keep you afloat....

A JOURNAL

◦◦◦ⓐ A gift for a special person who has arrived at a significant moment in their life! Treat yourself to an attractive sketchbook of a size you could take anywhere and a favourite pen and or pencil.

Mix up the sessions you have followed in this book and at least twice a week doodle with attention, creating a life-line amidst the turbulence. Be impulsive! Let spontaneity play upon your pages. Be childlike, carefree, joyous in your diary entries.

A HAPPY DIARY.

◦◦◦ⓑ Once every week, knowing the power of positive words and recalling bright events in your life, write what's termed a 'Gratitude Journal'. Start by revealing what's bothering you, end with a positive solution or a distraction or a good thing which happened recently.

GRATITUDE JOURNAL

◦◦◦ⓒ If written with sincerity, the 'Gratitude Journal' has a powerful but short lived effect, felt only for a week after the last entry, so weekly writing is advisable if you wish to maintain the momentum you have carefully built-up.

A quick mental brightening is experienced by traumatised individuals who have spent 15 minutes writing about their shock for only 5 days. In some experiments, little cuts were voluntarily inflicted and it was found that the wounds repaired 6x quicker amongst those who genuinely wrote about their feelings than amongst control groups who wrote about other things, such as sunsets.

During the first day, people can feel overly engrossed in their feelings. They are advised to keep going. By the second or third day they become more objective and less self-obsessed. As time passes, they come to see their problems in a more universal light. On the last day, they feel lighter.

In over 200 experiments around the world, 'gratitude' subjects reported that they were more alert and enthusiastic, that they slept better, had more energy and started to exercise more. They also felt they were progressing better towards their own personal goals.

A block of ice captures the emotions felt after being dropped by a woman. The church doodle on P. 125 was done later, when calm, collected and strong. You could do the same - start with a fine pencil, maybe go over it in ink.

∘ ∘ ∘ ⓔ SMILE!
This is your main job from today onwards, the rest is simply what you do with your time upon this extraordinary planet.

a mooo of cows

Various techniques are used in this rapid cow doodle.

We talked about slow exhaling stimulating the vagus system, we mentioned that holding your breath when working increases tension. Well, sorry to confuse things, but occasionally holding an inhale with gentle purpose is beneficial.

Having studied African runners, who mostly live at high altitude, long distance runners worldwide now practice the trick outlined here.

Twice (better 4x) a day, hold your full breath for a count of five to ten heart beats, (listen to your body). Feel the oxygen doing you good. Slowly let it out to ten beats. Repeat this five times.

Over three months, this exercise tricks the brain into believing you are living at altitude. You produce more red blood cells which carry more oxygen. The long out-breath stimulates extra vagal calming. You could add this to the 'Vagal' breathing used in Settling.

Deep breathing beneath a beret upon a mountain in the rain.

You can't force your mind to marvel, but you can prepare a marvel-friendly environment by Settling, vagal breathing, standing tall, re-living a bright memory. Or you could also add in active morning Settling.

Standing tall, legs apart, knees soft, breathe deep as you slowly stretch high. Pause, lungs full, sensually appreciate being alive. Feel balanced, alert, energised. Slowly release air, bending the knees, easing your arms down.

Say:
"I am unique, majestic, empathetic."

Repeat this three to six times, loosening the body, encouraging fresh oxygen to flow everywhere. End tall, suspended from your crown by an imaginary silver cord, sensing your posture, mental strength and sensually appreciative of the natural environment supporting you.

Based on a Chinese morning exercise, it nudges us from self-obsessive mindsets, directing our attention to the stunning world beyond our tiny puddles. Aware of the ever moving Now, we have the choice to relax and immerse ourselves in to its flow, or, if time-pressed, enhance our day by carrying a grain of it within us.

On difficult days, even when this doesn't work, continue, knowing it reinforces the positive mindset you've spent these precious weeks building.

It is helpful to occasionally tell yourself:

'I can improve my lot by taking charge of myself. My attitude and posture are good, I exercise sufficiently, I generate my own happiness and I understand that sincere empathy enhances my existence.'

 INTERDEPENDENCE

Remind yourself frequently that we are connected to everything. The breeze strokes our cheeks, soothes our ears. A gust moves our hair, thunder races our heart.

What we do affects everything around us. We are part of this life we take for granted, are as essential to it as the ants in the grass below and yes, the fluffy clouds above. Our voices rebound off the walls, what we flush down the sink reaches the river, the speed we drive adds to global pollution, imported goods cost the environment more than those produced locally, affecting the creatures around us, and all creatures are as vulnerable and as valuable as you and me, even bacteria.

If only to preserve ourselves, we ought to live as lightly as possible, respecting other people, respecting nature's fragility. Such an attitude arises from being able to empathise, which comes from an awareness of ourselves, the webs which surround us and our mental plasticity. By being outside our own self-oriented thoughts, we sense the importance of nature and learn to respect its every detail.

Doodling things around you ought to remind you of these inter-dependent relationships.

Thai monks smoking outside a temple.

oops, it's gone

Change starts to happen right here, just now, not on holiday or next week. Don't delay, this moment is fleeting, here but suddenly gone. Grab it and enhance your appreciation of life.

Time as measured by society is a construct. Before clocks, candles and dripping sand, time was measured by daylight. In equatorial Kenya where day and night are almost the same length year round, 7am is called the 1st hour, noon the 6th, sunset the 12th. Each pre-Industrial British town had its own hour until railways showed us that Plymouth's sunset occurred 20 minutes later than London's.

Even time in your head is elastic. A day flashes past the 40 year old, but hangs around the infant for whom it is 14,000 times longer, being a smaller proportion of their perceived lifespan.

This shows why, as we grow older, life feels far too short. Living with an awareness of your mortality and fragility enhances it, so don't miss your opportunity to Settle whenever you can.

that's it

the last extra… just a few doodles to contend with.

in the launderette.

There is no mystery, things are as clear as daylight.

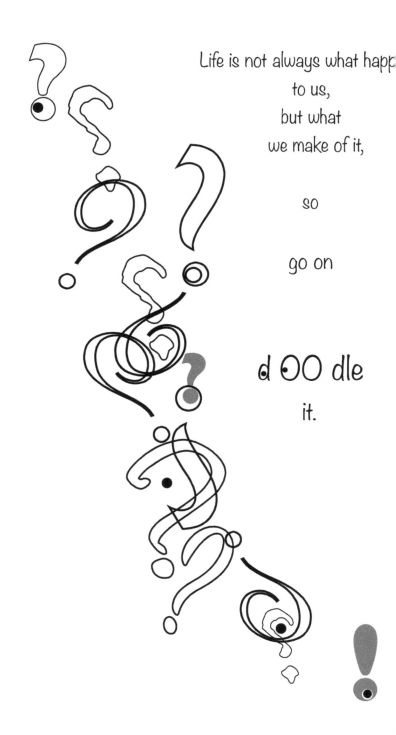

Life is not always what happ
to us,
but what
we make of it,

so

go on

d OO dle
it.

d O ⦿ d L e !

an eyeful

Just doodle away, enhancing your days

doing whatever turns you on...

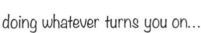

Take Note?

knowing it revives your 'soul', whatever that might mean...

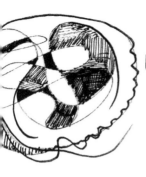

Keep doodling

without concern for quality.

Go on, you can ....

and be an idiot with abandon,

quickly scribble .....

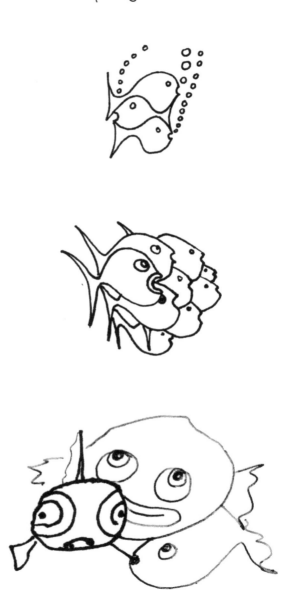

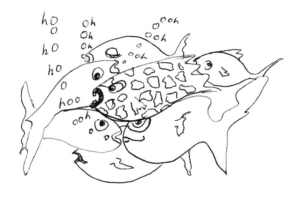

or pensively doodle

a squiggle of fish,

cartoons of a crowd,

imaginary faces

or real ones.

But which is which?

Who cares!

A flock of....

...No

a cloud of sheep

or a beret secret agent

Whatever you choose, the world is yours to doodle!

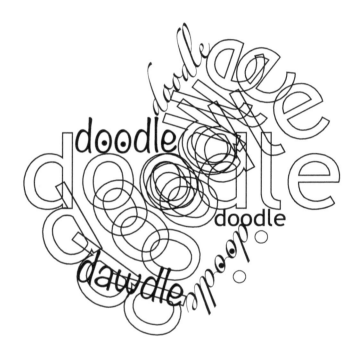

.... oh, just get on with it ...

.....if I must....

dOO dle !

"Life long satisfaction is gained from regular positive thinking about yourself, in sharing your happiest events with others and in savouring positive experiences."

Laura Kubzansky, Associate Professor,
Human Development and Health,
Harvard.

... in other words ...

dOOdle !

Why this book ?

Inspired by a noble Kenyan tribe, as I grew up my vision was at odds with my fellow colonialists who, unable to defeat them, appropriated that ancient people's fertile lands through deceit. Blessed with an extraordinary body and a fitness honed by playing with those athletic warriors, I felt anything was possible, yet unlike many in the tribe, I rejected the chance to be an Olympiad.

Discovering I had no passport, aged 21 I was forced to leave Kenya. Muddled, I worked and walked a quarter of the globe, befriending princes, bandits, rockstars, fools, millionaires, artists, gurus and fakes. I meditated, gained great peace, wanted to help others. Further education completed belatedly, rationalised me, civilised me, tamed my savage, unbroken self. But my lucidity faded. Bewildered, I conformed, fitted in, was successful, built castles.

When death, not once but several times, almost took me, my bounteous health fled forever. Depleted, denied much that I adored:-roaming wild terrain, working with others, dancing for hours, throwing parties, cooking elaborate dinners for friends, climbing, canoeing and much more, I had to adapt. Each day's start is grim, unable to cope my stress mounts. Gradually though, something tangible emerges; I call this process 'Settling'. Settling gave me the courage to hang-out with this new, weakened me, to draw, paint and write; to dwell in the better parts of myself.

Wishing to share the success of this process, I developed this system. Ensuring I wasn't blinded by hunches or myths, a reputed psychologist friend checked the book's scientific credibility. A talented artist-lecturer checked my doodling logic. I hope this system will lead you to accept yourself with all of your muck and shine and free you to Settle and touch your lyric self regularly.

And the beret obsession? In the French mountains berets are almost de rigeur; plus they are warm to boot.

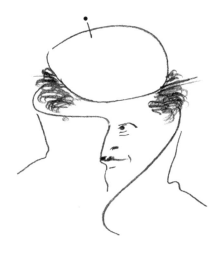

... that's it from me,

bye bye,

Iain

Thanks

My wife Millie - *endless* thanks for your forbearance, insightful editing and constant encouragement!

My thanks to Orla Cronin, a widely respected psychologist, you believed in this project and your scientific analysis of statements herein was invaluable.

David Dawson, poet, musician, troubadour, your inspiration helped the book evolve.

Retired art lecturer Colin Chambers, thank you for your advice.

Thanks also to personal counsellor Melanie Hammick and Reiki Master Sara Morley for checking this concept made wacky sense.

heartfelt thanks

REFERENCES

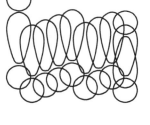

Ensuring this work's credibility, numerous scientific studies were referred to. Although an internet search will reveal research papers on topics in this book, on my website are some of the papers which helped me

- <u>iaindryden.com/books</u>
- & by this book's icon, tap on 'Research'.

Great Talks

The T.E.D. Talks website abounds with short, inspiring videos of experts in a variety of fields sharing their research or ideas.

Contact me
or

see more

iaindryden .com

Main font - Optima, 11
Headings & other - Gill Sans Light

Published Feb, 2020 by FeedARead.com Publishing.

Lightning Source UK Ltd.
Milton Keynes UK
UKHW010137120422
401412UK00001B/167

9 781839 452390